MI

Diary of a Lucky Zombie

Alex Brian

Table Of Contents

My name is Uhg, and I'm a zombie.

The life of a zombie is hard. We can never enjoy the sun. It's cramped underground. Wandering around aimlessly at night can get pretty boring.

It's not all bad, though. I'm the luckiest zombie I know. I don't have to run inside the second the sun starts to come up, because I have a nice leather hat. How many zombies can say that, huh?

Steve showed up about 2 weeks ago, and he's been building weird stuff. Maybe he's a nice guy though. I think I'll pay him a visit tonight.

Day 1:

He wouldn't let me in. I knocked, and knocked, and knocked on that big iron door.

I could see him through the slots in the door, and he looked right at me-- and ignored me!

He just sat in front of his furnaces, cooking steak and smelting iron ingots. Once he'd put all those things in, he went to bed. How rude.

I could see inside, though. He had a big picture of a creeper above his bed, but he wouldn't let them in either.

I stood outside for a long time, peering into his windows, looking at all his stuff. So fancy. Little flowerpots, all kinds of chests, a plush red bed, carpet.

He even grew a bunch of human food in a big building just beside his house. He sure works quick.

I met some new friends outside his house, though! We all hung around, waiting for him to come out in the morning.

They didn't look so happy, and I'm starting to see why. Maybe they tried to be friends once too, and he locked them out.

He's just like the villagers. We waited around as long as we could, but my friends had to go back to their caves and holes when the sun started coming up.

I stayed around a little longer, and a few of the creepers snuck into his pool to wait for him. Hehehe.

I can see him from my cave on the mountain. He's always shearing sheep, feeding cows, and planting human food.

I wonder if it's fun? I don't know if I like what he's doing to our valley, though. He already knocked down all the trees, and leveled the hills.

The creepers eventually got tired of waiting for him and left, and the second they were gone, he ran up and filled the pool in. Who does he think he is?

Day 2:

Today, my new skeleton friend
Tarsus and I decided to go down to
the abandoned mineshaft. He
brought his pet spider Archie, and
rode him around for hours.

You should've seen him climb! He
even showed us how he shoots his
bow while Archie's running around.
Steve won't know what hit him.

I found a weird room, though. It's dark, and there's a weird box in the middle. I decided to stay around for a little while, and now I've got lots of new zombie friends!

We like the same kinds of clothes, and love doing the same stuff.

When the sun went down, we all came out of the caves and scared Steve! He was fishing in the lake at the foot of the mountain.

You should have seen the look on his face when I snuck up behind him and said "uhg"! He started jumping around, fell into the water, and swam all the way back to his house.

So funny. We all stood outside till just before sunrise again, groaning and banging on his door. He eventually went to sleep, but it was still fun.

Day 3:

I don't think Steve was too happy about our shenanigans last night. I guess he saw where I went last night, because he started mining inside our mountain today.

It's not easy to relax when he's banging that pickaxe on the walls all day, you know!

Tarsus told me about a great place in the desert he saw a long time ago, but could never find his way back to.

After a few hours of wandering tonight, I found it! I told you I'm the luckiest zombie in the world. It's a big desert temple, with all kinds of pretty orange designs on the outside.

I hear it gets really bright during the day, but I'll be fine inside, especially with my trusty leather hat.

It was kinda weird though. On my way out, I saw this strange purple door. It was waving around and making weird noises, and I'm pretty sure Steve built it.

Maybe he built it out here because he didn't want to listen to that infernal noise all day. I can't blame him!

Day 4:

Hahaha! Steve came over today when it was bright outside. He walked right in like he owned the place and started with that pickaxe again, taking the sandstone from inside the temple.

In the middle of the main chamber, there's a great orange star with a blue center. I was watching from upstairs when he chopped right through the center and went plummeting down!

I heard a big boom, so I went to see what happened, but he was already gone. He left all his stuff down there, too!

All sorts of tools, and materials, all the sandstone he took, and a bunch of weird green orbs. I thought I might go down and get it all, but I couldn't figure out how to get down there without falling.

How would I get out then? No, I'm fine up here. It all disappeared after a little while anyway. He's so sneaky.

After the sun went down, I took a little tour of the desert. There's a great lava pool just a few minutes away, and a nice cave nearby.

I can't find another weird box room, but there are plenty of new friends here. Creepers, Skeletons, and Spiders. You can always count on them to help you out. Steve came back around, swinging his sword tonight.

Everybody helped out and sent him running back home, though. I have such great friends. It was so much nicer here before he showed up.

Day 5:

I get luckier every day, I swear.
Tarsus came by the temple tonight.

Apparently Steve's been going in and
out of that weird gate a lot and
bringing back strange white stones
and orange rods.

Anyway, Tarsus told me about

another great place - a village nearby. He said there were lots of new friends there, now that they'd busted all the doors down.

When I got there, I saw lots of big-nosed zombies walking around. All the buildings were wide open, so I shuffled around the blacksmith's shop for a while.

I found a really cool glowing golden helmet! The other zombies had already picked up the rest of the set and run off with them, but I'm happy to have a new helmet. The leather on the old one was getting a little scratchy anyway.

I found the cutest little zombie scampering around the village. He followed me home and everything.

I think I'll keep him, and call him Rargh. He can have my old hat when he's big enough to wear it.

Day 6:

What a weird day!

I put my helmet on and followed
Steve around today. I stayed way
back behind him so he wouldn't see
me, and tried to keep from groaning
and growling.

He had this weird thing, like a green

ball. Every time he threw it, it'd fly way up into the sky and fall, and then he'd run after it and pick it up.

Imagine my surprise, when he threw it and it went right down through the ground!

He pulled out a shovel, and started digging. A little while later, he came back up, building a ladder from bottom to top.

When he went back down, I decided to sneak down after him. I didn't do too bad, considering it was my first time climbing a ladder.

It was so strange down there. Crazy bugs kept coming out of some stones when he hit them with his pickaxe. There were so many!

There were some Skeletons and Endermen hanging around, but no one I knew. They seemed a lot meaner than the ones back in the mountain, too.

Steve put torches everywhere he went, and I could follow him easily enough that way. He went to a big library, and looked at a bunch of the books.

There was a place with a lot of weird cages too, but I don't know what it was for.

He ended up standing over this strange square thing with a bunch of holes in the top, but he didn't do anything with it.

I guess that's what he was looking for, because he built a ladder straight up from there and went home. Must have been in a hurry too, because by the time I got back to the original ladder, not wanting him to see me following, he was gone.

I almost went back to the mountain out of habit, but remembered that I live in the village now. Little Rargh was waiting for me when I got home.

I can't stop thinking about that thing, though. I feel really lucky that I got to see something almost no other zombies have, but it's still really weird.

Day 7:

Steve's been acting so weird lately. This morning, he set up this strange-looking building, and carried a bunch of bookshelves in.

He's been coming out with glowing stuff-- bows, swords, and armor, mostly. He's also started wearing a pumpkin on his head, and I'm not sure why.

The Endermen seem to ignore him when he does. They're so weird.

I wonder if he's okay? He seems so serious. He almost looked like he was having fun before.

Day 8:

Nothing really big happened today. Steve mostly stayed in his house, moving stuff between boxes, forging a bunch of pickaxes, making them glow somehow in that building.

I think he's getting ready for a trip back to that weird place. I can see the big tower he built by it from here, lined with all those torches.

He picked up all of his human plant food and thinned out his herd to make a bunch of steak too. While I was watching, I noticed something really strange. I think he was wearing the same clothes I was.

Why didn't I ever notice that? How bizarre. You know, all the zombies wear the same outfit, come to think of it.

Is Steve some different kind of

zombie? Maybe we were Steves before. What does that mean? Maybe I was supposed to do what he's doing, and didn't quite make it.

If that's the case, I'm pretty lucky. Whatever he's trying to do seems like it's going to be really hard. Maybe it's best that I'm a zombie, now. I have great friends, a great hat, and a little Rargh at home.

Day 9:

I went back to Steve's house tonight to see what he was up to. He was sleeping in his armor, and he got up the moment the sun was in the sky.

I followed behind him just like I did before, all the way up to that weird square. He put a bunch of those green balls into the slots, and I couldn't believe what I saw.

This big black portal popped up between the squares. It was smoking, and smoldering, and it looked like there was something really strange just past it. He waited for just a second, then jumped right through.

I can't stop thinking about our clothes, though. It can't be a coincidence. I'm sure of it, now. I was definitely a Steve before.

For some reason, this is what Steves are supposed to do. I'm kinda glad I'm not a Steve anymore, though. It looked pretty scary.

Steve never came back to his house after that. I wonder if he found what he was looking for in that portal? Maybe he moved into a new house there.

It's weird, not seeing him around, but I'm glad he got to do what he was supposed to. I'm glad I didn't have to, too. I'm happy here in my village with my friends and Rargh.

I guess I'm lucky to be just who, what, and where I am.

Preview Of Diary Of A Minecraft Creeper

Day 1

I think I was born today! The first creepy memory I have is of my heartbeat, a faint ticking sound beneath my chest.

I couldn't feel it, I do not have arms. Hey, wait a second...I don't have ears either... But I could certainly hear it! It was so creepy.

I saw my reflection in a little pond nearby, black holes for eyes and a crooked smile. I truly was a Creeper.

Ahead of me, I saw a vast landscape of trees and grass. Confused as to what my purpose was, I listened closer to my heartbeat.

Tick, Tick, Tick. I am unsure how I just appeared here or what I should do. This is all just so creepy, I feel like wandering around in circles until I find a real purpose.

This is my diary, the Diary of A Creeper. I have decided that since today is the day I was born, today would be my Birthday.

Happy Creepy Birthday to me! I should write down everything I know, like a memoir. I will walk in circles the rest of the night until I figure out what I should do next.

[Click Here To Read 'Diary Of A Minecraft Creeper'](http://amzn.to/1DX87BK)

Or Go To: http://amzn.to/1DX87BK

Made in the USA
Lexington, KY
27 June 2015